T0064061

THE
CRIMSON
Sky

THE
CRIMSON
Sky

The Consumed Quota of Life

PALITHA RANATUNGE

PARTRIDGE

To order additional copies of this book, contact
Toll Free 800 101 2657 (Singapore)
Toll Free 1 800 81 7340 (Malaysia)
orders.singapore@partridgepublishing.com

www.partridgepublishing.com/singapore

CONTENTS

(1) Time 1

(2) The Freedom Fighter 2

(3) The Grave Yard 4

(4) The Spider Friend 5

(5) Guilt 7

(6) The Migrant 8

(7) Waiting for Justice 10

(8) The Ascetic 12

(9) The Crows 14

(10) Bother Not Please 16

(11) Pinocchio 18

(12) The Chicken 20

(13) Abortion 22

(14) The Civil Act 24

(15) The Rapist 25

(16) The Kashyapa of Sigiriya 26

(17) The Cockroach 29

(18) Political Asylum Seekers 31

(19) The Birds 33

(20) Ingratitude 34

(21) The Emptiness 35

(22) Humans 36

(23) The Sickness 37

(24) Fortune Teller 39

(25) I am Rip Van Winkle 40

(26) The Lost 42

(27) The Perfect Love 43

(28) My Loneliness 45

(29) My Love 46
(30) The Little Mermaid's Love.............................. 47
(31) The Sleep Walker......................................51
(32) The Souvenirs of Love 52
(33) Unattendedness 53
(34) Fear and Wisdom 54
(35) Pandora's Box...55
(36) Perplexity Before the Truth...................... 57
(37) The Mirrors 58
(38) Transcendent the Humanity 59
(39) The Love 62
(40) The Truth...65
(41) Killing of a Self...................................... 67
(42) The Sinner.. 69
(43) Pray for Thy Betterment 71
(44) Contentment 73
(45) The Quota...74
(46) The Mind.. 76
(47) The Rain, the Same One 78
(48) Death Wish of a Poet............................... 80
(49) The Crimson Sky...................................... 82

(1)

Time

I have worshipped many a god
Who were not kind to me
My trust on *karma* or fate
All nothing but words
Just a few guidelines,

I am only a biological unit
Born to grow, fade and die
If you are inquisitive
Learn now who would be
The mightiest of all
Never be late to fade the life in your eyes
Never be late to discolour the paint on your lips
Even to take the memories in your brain cells,

Dinosaur, Alexandor, Ceasor and Ashok
Homer, Shakespeare, Kalidas and Tagore
Moses, Buddha, Jesus, and Mohammed
All the greatest taken away by one
Who is impartial and merciless
The ruler of the universe
The mightiest of all.

Karma- is the law of moral causation. This belief was prevalent in India before the advent of Buddha. Nevertheless, it was the Buddha who explained and formulated this doctrine in the complete form.

(2)

The Freedom Fighter

A long time ago when I was a small child
I caught a bird, a bird of brown feathers
Tiny blue sparkling eyes around its short beak
I caught it after hours of struggle,

I put it in a cage made of wood
And gave the bird many a food and purest water to drink
On the following morning I noticed
It was dying, shivering with utmost pain
With eyes and beak soaked with blood,

It had knocked and knocked
Its tiny head against the thickness
Of the hard wooden walls
And killed itself leaving all my care,

I was puzzled and sad
Why he did it, though I gave him
A nice cage to live, sweetest food to eat
Purest water to drink,

I enquired from my mother
Why it wanted to kill itself
And I was told, fear of death
It died, knocking its head
Against the thick wooden walls,

No mother, it was not the reason
After many a year today
I know why it killed itself,
It died of fear of losing
The freedom of life,
Because there was no use
Of living without it.

The Grave Yard

Everyday I pass by you
I was fascinated by
The beauty of you,

In wintry mornings
You are covered with
Milky velvet,

In blossoming spring
You are garlanded with
Green grass,

In shining summer
You are laden with
Lilies and roses,

In windy fall
You are hidden with
Dead leaves,

At all times you are calm
And caring the dead
Underneath your soft
Everlasting embrace
On their decaying cells.

(4)

The Spider Friend

You have spun a beautiful web
Trapping insects passing by
Shutting off the stunning vision
At my bedroom window,

Hours at my leisure
I gaze through your net
At the garden below
Where flowers sway their
Colored heads, tossing in the breeze
Bathing in glittering sunlight,
Where humming birds sing
Music holding their colored
Nectar cups at their buffet
Having brunches and lunches,

Why should I break your
Little fortress
Since you also a part of
My world
Why shouldn't I adore
The magnificence of your
Architecture, craftsmanship,
Huntsman ship, geometrical and
Symmetrical correctness,

And becoming admirable
And humble in looking through
Your beautiful fortress
The beauty of my garden
With utmost amazement,
And an enhancing adoration
Towards you and the others.

(5)

Guilt

A little green grass hopper
At the door of my office . . .
A fortunate one, indeed!
Not to get trampled
By a passer-by,

With great care
I took it on my palm
And reconnoiter for a green
To place him in protection
Alas! No such green around,

In my little sky scrapper,
I went in and placed him
On a book shelf in my room,
Having a little break in work
I looked for the friend,

Alack! it was down on the floor
Like a green pulp, trampled
By my own shoe and died
Unnoticed and spontaneous . . .
Oh! My folly and my fault
And I got him killed in vain!

(6)

The Migrant

I am displaced like a tropical tree
newly planted in an icy land
the very sensitive edges of
its roots cannot adjust to
The coarseness of the hard soil,

The manure and water are bitter
Having no homely air to breathe
The coldness in the night unbearable
And other plantations around
Genetically mutated and artificial
Not friendly or sensitive at all,

No familiar birds, butterflies or little squirrels
No laughter, love and affection around
No sweeter melodies of gentle breeze
Carrying the fragrances of distant flowers
Blooming and hidden within green mountains.
I have been desperate for salvation
Similar to the sufferings of *Dick Wittington*
Who had fled for green pastures in London
Dreaming of the streets made of gold
And houses made of diamonds and people
Who only ate chocolate cream?

This is not rewriting a fairy tale, for
There will be no masters with such kindness
There will be one eyed cats to be sold
For half a kingdom and of course, no such
Foolish kings around offering such prizes,

Nor will there be Royal dinners where
Rats play hell on the dining tables,
The Big Ben would be dumb for a poor migrant . . .
Ben only sings at Royal Weddings
There will be no such fair elections for such
An unknown to become the Mayor of London.

Dick Wittington – Dick Wittington and His Cat is the name of English
folklore surrounding the real – life Richard Wittington (c. 1354-1423),
wealthy merchant and later Lord Mayor of London, telling a story of how
he supposedly escaped his poverty-stricken childhood and made his fortune
thanks ratting abilities of his cat.

(7)

Waiting for Justice

The moon fades
The bat goes and
Crickets are chirping
A melody of daylight
That embraces tree barks,

Still no sun peeped
Over the eastern shades
Of the green lines of
The tree Kingdom far away
In the misty wilderness,

A huge soft carcass of
A tusker lay motionless
Without a single tusk
His coarse skin is covered
With black ants and blue flies . . .

The dead has to be removed
By the forest by itself according to
A set of funeral rituals
A tiger, jackal, monitor or a vulture
Has the right for such,

None has appeared, I wonder?
Still the tiger to come!
Still the jackal to come!
Still the monitor to come!
Still the vulture to come!

Well, they may have determined
Not to disturb the crime scene
By tampering evidence of the kill
Foot prints of the mercenaries
Who fearless of their conscience,

They are not to damage
The blood soaked bullet wounds
Still warm with the pain of the animal
Made by the thundering rifle shots
On the majestic skull of the king,

(8)

The Ascetic

The man walks passing by
Every day and night
In rain and in hot sun wearing
A shabby and lousy coat
Covering a little of him,

His face shaved, but
Weary of no sleep at night
His search for something
Missing from his life
May be our life as well,

We do not have the time
For this journey of finding . . .
He searches repeatedly
Searching for the same
But unknown to us
May be he knows.

Sometimes I encounter him
At the pavement of a dark corner
He stands still gazing at nothing
Deep in thought with mysterious
Bliss in his eyes,

You might say it's the pain
But I always believe, it as
A great bliss of achievement
Of the status so called
That can be attained
By only an ascetic
In a sacred and secret life,

I know you cannot transform
Your bliss into words and letters
And circulate among us
Who have still been loitering
Around, at the same place . . .
Pursuit of happiness
Believing blindly the present day
Asian and Middle-Eastern mythologies.
Have you ever been determined
In exploring for any such truth
In our characterless neighborhood?

(9)

The Crows

Cry aloud, with their shrieking voices
Jarring the morning air, invited by
A maid who feared the God *Senasuru*
Since he has cursed upon her
To get his crew of crows fed,

The squirrel mother hides her little ones
In the branches of a neighboring tree.
Fear of killers clouded the morning light
With their doomed black fury,

Other colored bird, a *Koha*
Prevents singing of her arcadian
Morning melodies fearing the
Rioters, rioting for bread crumbs
Fallen one by one from the
God fearing maid, praying for
an evasion and salvation from
Senasuru maha dasava,

Having no depth in mind, the one
Who advised the poor maid
To feed the children of Nature
Only misbalancing their food cycles
Is a true enemy of Mother Nature.

God Senasuru- He is called god of Saturn as well.

Sensauru Maha Dasava – If Saturn is well placed, it brings honor, authority and prosperity. In case it is afflicted, the time period brings major difficulties, calamities, sorrows and frustrations.

Koha- is an Indain plaintive who sings beautifully.

(10)

Bother Not Please

A bitch, a dog mother
Doesn't lay eggs but puppies.
Likewise the other domestic pet
The mother cat,
Though they lay high in number
We lay only one rarely two
And three miraculously.
But in their case they give
Birth to more expecting only
One or two to survive,
Alas! Thanks to medical science
We have managed to save our
Almost all the offspring . . .
Yet, it was not the bright idea
Of nature, the all mighty mother,

Hence you need not be troubled and cry for
All the puppies and kittens at and around
Our home, road side pavements
Or at unattended garbage bins.
Be at ease letting them
Survive in accordance with the
Natural law of earth,
Torrents of rain in a cold night
Hot sun or a screeching car tire
Will do the balancing process,

On the other hand, do not forget
And be little wise at least to think
They became domestics because of
Our fault and they have been our
Tamed slaves trained to act as
Watchers, companions, daughters, sons etc.,

Having no right to object to their impersonation
Having nowhere to go,
These poor so called pets of ours
Do not belong to our artificial home life
Or the free world of far away wilderness.

(11)

Pinocchio

Blue fairy where art thou?
I pray for thy blessings
For my son, whom I made
Of wood. I being the carpenter
and the creator like
Joseph in Israel,
With thy magic wand
Give it life, form of a child
We both have no hope
Of an offspring of our own
At our poor dwelling,
Having tired of preaching at
All the altars of many Gods,

When I remembered about
Thy existence in ancient
Europe, somewhere close to
The land of Grimm brothers,
Hence, I pray for thy magic
Do tell us where thou are chambered

To pay our respectful visit and seek
A life for our wooden child
Made by my own hand
With such pain, care and hope.

Pinocchio- is a fictional character and the protagonist of the children's novel
"The Adventures of Pinocchio" (1883), by the Italian writer Carlo Collodi.

(12)

The Chicken

I encountered them
Bundled in a tiny iron cage
At the poultry seller.
All were feeble and hungry
Pale fear in their eyes
Having seen the mates
Chopped up every minute
One by one, just like in
'Apocalypto'
Of Mel Gibson,

I wanted to save them all,

Well, you can save them
By buying them all and
Feeding them until
A comfortable death.
Tell me is it worth
Giving these factory made

Broiler friends a future?
Since they are only manufactured
For KFC or Mc Donald paper boxes,

Pity? isn't it?

Apocalypto – is a 2006 American epic adventure film directed and produced
by Mel Gibson. It was written by Gibson and Farhad Safinia.

(13)

Abortion

Forgive me, my darling
I also have conspired
With them to kill you,
They all wanted your blood,
Your death, they all fear
Your birth, your growth,

I have been beaten
I have been tormented
I have been forced
To give my consent
To enforce a death warrant
On you, my love,

I have been reasoning
I have been weeping
I have been fighting
For your life for I had felt
Your palpitating soft blood
Running through my feeble veins.
But all efforts were worthless
My motherhood all alone
Was defeated before
The well being of a cultured
Society, it gives permission
To sin but not in public,

I had been with chained hands
No way out of my prison cell
I myself, with the others as well
Ones who had forced me
Had strongly believed that
They were the true guardians,

Their sins are respectable
And unquestionable.
The tradition that they have
Worshipped for their own benefit
Is a flower basket on a
Well covered sewage pit,

I am one of the virgin mothers
Who tempted by a sincere embrace
For wink of a second,
I was vulnerable,
Oh! Why their God had acted
In such a hurry in his so called
Graceful process of creation.

(14)

The Civil Act

What is beyond this optimum?
Can I not stop this flowing second?
Sweetness of moaning pulses
Of stars uncounted glimpses
Set fire to every red cell circulating,

The abundance of love overflowing,
Has driven away the repulsion
And the sickness in the stomach
The continuing stamina is emerged
As another deep sacrifice in the heart,

The palpitations that have not arisen
From the primodial animal instincts,
The fear of losing this limited harmony,
The wild desire in embracing the sensation
The floating seconds resting in heaven,

Animals cannot play such tones
Harmonized with blood red roses
It's the man made art of war
Throughout the generations
Deviating from primary forms.

(15)

The Rapist

Hey, may I whisper unto thy soul
And pour the pure liquid of my
Budding love unto thy virgin heart?
Feeling inexperienced palpitations
Presenting such an exotic warmth
Beyond the cradle of childhood
Since the day of thy attainment,

Ay, 'tis a mistake, a fatal one
Ye despised my true confessions
Of melancholy that swells and sobs
With dismal and pure anger
Pushing my lost soul unto an insanity
And transforming me to a werewolf,

Oh! dear one, do not make public my crime
Do forgive my emptiness and my folly
Knowing not the irony of practical life
Of civilization that has been manipulated
Our true impulses and compulsions for mating
Into such a dirtiness and codified intrusion.

Werewolf – it is also called Lycanthropy. The word Lycanthropy comes form
Greek, lykoi, "wolf" and anthropos, "man". It is a human with the ability
to shape shift into a wolf like creature.

(16)

The Kashyapa of Sigiriya

You have left your
Uniqueness to be captured
With great respect and gratitude
Through out centuries
Appreciated deeply
In future, the time immemorial
And Centuries ahead,

You are a man, we would love to
Imagine according to our perceptions
You must have been handsome
Young, strong and flexible
To living in such a mountain trek
With all entertainment around
For a real man and a king,

In spite of all grandeur
Having all the skills available
You have left out something
To be monumental and precious
For the future as done by other kings
As a gift from historical grandeur
A statue or a picture of your grace,

Maybe it reveals the simplicity
Of you and appreciation for
Only the art and its value
Not like other kings who had
Been promoting nothing
But their self and selfishness
Tampering true pages of history,

Hence you being invisible
In our hearts filling full respect
But you being invincible
Throughout generations
As the noblest King of
Ancient Seegiriya kingdom
Fifteen hundred years ago,

And the most valiant Commandant
At warfare having courage to
Kill yourself before the shame of
Defeat, showing the world the
Utmost dignity of an invincible pride
In a lion heart, not the cowardice
Having left all loved ones at the palace,

Having such bravery and dignity in heart
I doubt the history as to your patricide
You may have been deported to a forest
Far from your flawed inheritance,
The history is the deeds of man
But not a manipulation by fake historians
Disgracing the greatness with great lies,

Can anybody witness such evidence?
As to a repentance of a man who
Committed such patricide?
Who hid himself for fear of death?
I can gather only a taste of a sensitive
Man with great self esteem, creativity and
Courage with most precious kind of simplicity.

Kashyapa of Seegiriya - Kashyapa 1, also known as Kasyapa 1, was a king of Sri Lanka, who ruled the country from 473 to 495 CE. Kashyapa is credited with the construction of the Sigiriya Citadel and the surrounding city.

(17)

The Cockroach

You have been living for
Billions of years
Before us mammals,
Being a true descendant
Of mighty *Trilobite*
Who had been trotting
In the ancient water world
In the mysterious era
Of Pre-Cambrian,

Today you play a game
Of hiding and seeking
A game of death for
Mere permission to live in
Our sophisticated dwellings
Cornered into the darkness
And be a squatter in damp
Tiny holes that have been
Filled with terror and death,

You have been harmless
To our species throughout
The last millions of years
You have not been the reason
For any human pestilence,

Rats for the plague
Mosquitoes for dengue and others
Bugs for blood sucking
But you for nothing,

You only nibble a remnant
On a dish at a kitchen table
Or scaring a delicate female
In spite of your weak character
Yet you have survived
Before many strategically planned
Warfare at our household
Armed with sophisticated
Chemical weaponry,

You are much despised
And unwelcomed by us
In such invulnerableness
You may live a longer life,
Even after the extinction of
Our species, humans
Being a diplomat of all ages
On this planet earth
Growing up to be a leader.

Trilobite – Long before the fish inhabited the seas and Dinosaurs roamed the land, Trilobites appeared some 600 million years ago during the Cambrian period. They evolved rapidly into many beautiful, bizarre and even by today's standards, futuristic forms.

(18)

Political Asylum Seekers

Why my love, carrying a biological weapon?
Why not realize
Every such attempt will be an unsuccessful mission?
They are not domestics
Like a rat, bug or a cockroach,

Why a little brat gecko on the wall
Dwells on the dining table and suburbs
Licking our curry bowls and bread crumbs?

Why a filthy frog crept in to the kitchen
Bumping itself on the cleaned floor
Inviting a serpent into the house?

Why a stinking bat laid filth
Right on the car bonnet every morning
Giving an unpleasantness?

Why these miserable ants marching
Parades unto every corner of the house
Searching for a left over of any kind?

Oh! dear, we cannot prevent
Them from coming
The truth is that these dwellings
We claim exclusively as ours
Actually are not ours, it's theirs as well,

We have invaded and inhabited
Their ancestral lands
Their territories forever
Well, will that be? I doubt
It's only, until our extinction!

Having no force to fight back
Or to organize a systematic
Guerilla warfare, they just lay
Feeble, isolated and meek
Looking at us but with limitless fear,

Creeping a little into our comforts
They seek only a little food to eat
And a small shelter to breed and feed
Safe from their predators day and night,

They still seek shelter pleading
Mercy at our forbidden lands
Knowing that we do not
Well, at least for the time being
Kill, fry or boil and eat them.

(19)

The Birds

I look at the birds that dwell on the sky
Singing happy songs fluttering with the breeze
With colorful feathers, eyes and beaks,

Oh! Have I ever thought
That they are the angels?
Who are said to live in heaven?
Well, logically not incorrect,

They are soft, light and beautiful
And everlastingly cheerful
Moreover they live above us all
Flying high, always mingled
And smitten with sweet fragrance
Of the flowers and fruits
Those that are hidden on tree tops
Of windy far away mountains,

They have no limits, and boundaries
Their limit is one and only, the sky
Believe me that they are the real angels
Most privileged and most fortunate.

(20)

Ingratitude

Monkeys, birds and bears
Hanuman, Jatayu and Jambuwan
Fought with Rama
Against the evils of
Demon king Ravana,

Amazingly Rama and his brother
Were the only humans
Fought in the historic war
For the salvation of mankind,

Today, after many thousands of years
Have you ever been shown any sense
Of gratitude towards the
Said allies?

Rama- is the seventh avatar of the Hindu god Vishnu. Rama is also the protagonist of the Hindu epic Ramayana, which narrates his supremacy.

Hanuman- was a monkey and a great warlord who fought with prince Rama against Ravana.

Jatayu – was a huge bird who fought bravely with Ravana and gave its life when Ravana was abducting the princess Sita, the beloved wife of prince Rama.

Jambuwan – was a bear and a great warlord who fought with prince Rama against Ravana.

(21)

The Emptiness

A man of fifty years
Gazed at the beauty of
A starry night,
First time in his life.

(22)

Humans

I met him by the road side
Wearing shabby clothes
And selling living parrots
Holding a cage filled with
A few green beauties
Hugging each other
Looking eagerly
At the same greenery
We all belonged to,

I said I wanted a parrot
To be released
And asked him

"Tell me the price"
What he said was
Wonderful to hear
For you all,

"Sir, if it is for releasing
I charge half price"

Was he above us all
Wasn't he?

(23)

The Sickness

Nay, I never wanted it
From thou in return for
What I offered, I being
Dumb and a failure
I loved you, but no
Return, I loved the love
For the sake of loving,

I wanted to love
And not to be loved
If you say you are in love
Madly with me, definitely
I would leave you
For, I am desperate
And mentally ill,

I am like a serial killer
Who cannot live without killing
I am like a thief
Who cannot live without stealing
I am like an alcoholic
Who cannot live without drinking,

I am addicted to love
I am addicted to perfection
I am addicted to honesty
I am addicted to sacrifice,

I wanted myself to be burnt
Within the fire of love and
Suffer, hence never worry
About the destiny of mine
Never take it as a burden
Just pass by ignoring me,

As an accident victim laid
Unattended in the midst of a busy town
Until the undertaker comes
You never endure the least worry
Just pass by ignoring me.

(24)

Fortune Teller

When I was wandering alone
With the old sun
Who peeps over the
Deserted dead end
Of the long footpath,
I met a man with a
Wrinkled face – a fortune teller
Insisting of
Telling my fortune
For just one penny
I said nay and asked him
Not to be dismal.
Do tell me what fortune
I am to be entitled
Except expecting
An endless but sound sleep
In one final morning
After a one cold night.

I am Rip Van Winkle

I slept a little on the soft grass
In the magic mountain
Can you remember my name?
I am Rip Van Winkle,

My heart is full of love
May I touch your soft fingers
And express my heart's agony?
Will you look at my eyes
With your trembling lips?

Will you murmur the same
Half spoken words
Hey! where are you looking at?
I am here just sitting opposite
Pleading for your hand
As I did then, can't you remember?

I have been dreaming
In my deep sleep
I was bound by a magic spell
My body may have decayed
But my heart is the same,
Oh! Can't you see me?
Can't you hear me?

Can't you feel me?
Can't you remember me?
I am Rip Van Winkle
Am I to be ignored?

Rip Van Winkle – it is a short story by American author Washington Irvin published in 1819. He was inspired by German folklore in writing this story. The general plot of the story is a man who mysteriously sleeps for 20 years to find himself in a changed world.

(26)

The Lost

The sighs of loneliness
Did you hear not?
A life without wine and women
Is a bore
Said the bar keeper with
A sly grin.
A star winked at my window
Seeing my emptiness
I sighed for the nostalgia
I wonder who sings the same
Loving tunes of the past
I shout at you lark
Do shut thy black lips
'Cos my love is laid
With the by-gone days.

Lark – A bird having a melodious song, especially a skylark. It is particularly
noted for its rich, sustained song and for singing in the air.

(27)

The Perfect Love

I was at the window in the long nights
Watching you growing and fading . . .
One day I was happy to look at your
Full moon face, the other days
You were fading into pitch darkness,

Leaving me all alone, in the darkness
Of the mighty universe, having
No one to share the life
In all tomorrows of the past,

I admired your unique beauty
And felt your kindness
In every palpitation of my heart
But I felt all at once the reality
And your non-existence,

I dreamt in the night, embracing
Your heart
Crying indeed for nothing, may be
The sweetest odour of your soul
Pierced in to my bones
Like the freezing wind
Blowing at snow capped mountains
Like those picturing in a movie,

My love was with perfection
Of womanhood
That had been created by me
In my dreams far from
The reality of life
Hence I am at the window
Looking at the dark night
Painting a symbol of perfect love
That could never have existed.

(28)

My Loneliness

The rainbow in the sky
Sparkling colours over my head
Short meetings and happiness
I dare not look away
For it goes a wink of time,

I hugged a beautiful dream
Thinking that it was eternal
Cried for love and care
It was a dead wink of time
You pass by as a stranger,

Your survival was eternal and
Content without my love
I could not sleep a single night
The heart is feeble and weak
Can it bear such a blow?,

The world is old and weary
The rainbow in the sky
Gone as feared by me
All in my inward eye is empty,
Dull and monotonous.

(29)

My Love

You have to catch my inward eye
When I throw away the sorrows of life
The entrance to the cave of eternity
With eternal happiness of nullity
When you weep in deep thinking of me
My dumbness gives you an enlightenment
The life ahead will lead to prosper,

The way I lead my life rich with kindness
Simplicity and contentment
Find you the pathway to success
Shall change your destiny to real
Come, grab my hand and be independent
Temples, shrines and candles useless
But give you false hope for the future,

Past, present and future is the same
The difference is in you, fading your body
From youth to death unto nothingness
But brain has no limits it never fades
With growing confidence in truth
Fights confidently until the end, like a warrior
Dies without leaving the battle field.

(30)

The Little Mermaid's Love

Little mermaid, I bow my head
For your greatest sacrifices
For the sake of love,
May be in your mermaid kingdom
Hidden beneath thousand fathoms
Deep in a secret sea bed
True love existed in its true form
But in our world of humans
It's only a day dream longing in
Soft, virgin teenage hearts,

Such feeble apprentices of life
May write poems of love on
Beautiful and delicate rose petals
Singing softly the hymns of love,
When many combinations of
Egos of complex human minds
Self comes first and defeat divinity
Hence truth comes first
Converting the purest tears of love
To a kind of acid water when
Encountered with self oriented
betrayals unique to mankind,

Dear little mermaid, the beautiful
Daughter of great and powerful
Poseidon, the ruler of the mighty
And deepest seven seas,
Such had done to you by your
Prince beloved, heir to the
Mighty throne of *Atlantis*
You lost your unique blue hair
In exchange at the hands of a
Crooked legged black witch who
Offering you the most beautiful legs
Every lass would be dreaming of,

The ball at the grand palace
Has taken away his disguise
As any prince in the world
Your one has betrayed your love
And crippled your purest soul
As soft as glacier water drops
Silently falling at silent hours
At a far away snowy mountain edge,

The day of your sorrow
Has doomed the hearts of
Every virgin lover on earth
The lost feeble soul of you
Fallen into the same sea
Where you came out of
Its icy coldness had swiftly
Embraced the scattered
Limbs of your soft body,

Transforming its utmost beauty
And neurotic sense of love
Into thousand bubbles of
Cold, bitter and dumb sea water
Taking you into an eternal slumber
Deep deeper deepest in the sea,

Well, from that day of sacrifice
The whole sea is weeping
Every day at every sea shore
On this planet earth
Whispering meekly a sad but lovely
Farewell song for all
Who hath killed themselves
For the sake of love
On this mighty earth, on, beneath and over,

You my friend, I invite you to be at a sea shore
Wherever in the world at a melancholy
And silent night to share her song of the moan
Singing together with thousands of sea waves
Together with the followers of our little
Mermaid princess having embraced her folly
Deep deeper deepest in heart with an
Admiration for the creator of such a beautiful
Fairy tale, that has the quality to be an
Everlasting memory in any sensitive heart
That has sensed a true love.

Little Mermaid – is a fairy tale by the Danish author Hans Christian
Anderson about a young mermaid willing to give up her life in the sea and

her identity as a mermaid to gain a human soul and the love of a human prince.

Atlantis – Legend says that Atlantis city was built by Poseidon, god of sea. However, the new researches have revealed a new site and the scientists are sure that Atlantis can be found in Cadiz, somewhere between the Spain and Morocco waters.

(31)

The Sleep Walker

'Tis a sleep walker
Who unknowingly
Turns the dark knobs
Of the secret chambers
Of the heart of thee
At most unwelcome hours
Fear not, 'tis not a day dream
May be the sweetest in a
Lonely night,

It may sigh, pray, cry
And open thy virgin heart
Shedding the blood purest
Cos unattended love
Shall die in a wink of time
Like a dew drop in a summer day,

It wakes up and goes
Becoming most unfamiliar
Hence be wise and be haste
Embracing the falling stars
At the far cloud's end
In the sweetest but shortest
Dreams of thee.

(32)

The Souvenirs of Love

Dear friend, today I call you
Yesterday I called you, my love!
While you were away beyond the seas
Our past is a tombstone at the
Grave yard yonder; inviting me to
Re- read the days gone by,

My suspicions at your soft touches
For I was not touched in my heart,
An ache deep in my soul still moans
Counting the silent but flying seconds
For my sacrifices of life expecting
A reincarnated love beyond the seas

The flowers you brought into my chamber
Have been beautiful and radiant
If instead you had brought the natural
Would have perished a long time back
Artificial are beautiful passing many a summer
In spite of missing any ambrosial scent.

(33)

Unattendedness

When I've grappled thee unto my heart
Thou still mourn for his dismissal
Why didst thou not die at his corpse?
Romeo, the murderer of himself and others
Years ago in a graveyard in ancient *Verona,*

Preventing me today from miseries of love
A true love burns deep in my heart
Swells than that of him, full of sacrifices too
Why do not thee feel mine at all
Thou art blind with lack of wisdom,

Juliet, my love where is thy dagger
Soaked with blood witnessing a sacrifice
Do present it to me for killing myself
Sacrificing my life for an unattended love.

Romeo and Juliet – is a tragedy written by William Shakespeare early in
his career about young star-crossed lovers whose deaths ultimately reconcile
their feuding families.

(34)

Fear and Wisdom

Man has a brain
Comparatively a big one
Wise he has been very much
Too much for himself
The others do have
But only for the needs
Of nature,

What to do with these
Excessive departments
Of human brain
They being wise but
More being scared of
The death unavoidable,
The dead cannot come back
And tell you their whereabouts
Then the man assumes
Phantoms and nonsense
And spends days and nights
Praying for a better after life,

Alas and alack! All based on
Mere guesswork
And repents all by himself
Compensating for his
Great wisdom gifted by
Excessive brain cells.

(35)

Pandora's Box

Pandora, the daughter of *Zeus*
Beloved wife of *Epimethus*
The wise and kind brother
Of Great God, *Prometheus*
Opened the secret box
Full of ugly creatures
Who were to represent all the
Ill feelings of mankind,

The day of her disobedience
Was the victory of the evil
Among human race on earth
But subject to one option
Because her wisdom and
Power of judging the good
From the bad, she had released
The final creature of the Lord,

Little but strong, meek but
Immortal, the true messenger
Of the holy kingdom of Olympus
The 'Hope', the rectifier
Of the agonies of human being
After being tortured by
The said ugly creatures
Sickness, hatred, greed, jealousy . . .,

The man for generations living with
The said "Hope" for betterment,
The King and/or the Priest
Has forced to evolve the said "Hope"
On to different destinations
Creating fantasies beyond
The death of a man enhancing
The hope for the said rulers' benefit.

Pandora – was the very first woman who was formed out of clay by the gods according to the Greek Mythology.

Prometheus – was a titan had originally been assigned with the task of creating man.

Zeus – was the king of gods, the god of sky and weather, law and order and fate.

(36)

Perplexity Before the Truth

When a man is doped with his belief
He is full of fantasies and false hopes
He is reluctant to gain consciousness
He is blind before the truth and logic
He is scared of the existentialism,
He seeks assistance from other cults
Though they teach different fantasies
And offering different destinations,
They all become allies, in attacking
The common enemy of fantasy,

With the false hope and the dope
He anticipates a rebirth to be with
His own clan and the own land
The other seeks eternal salvation
In the land above of the Creator,

He shuts down his conscience
And fears any word against such
Salvations, in the form of enhanced
Humanity in a rebirth, eternal divinity
or bliss in the heaven or *Nirvana*.

Nirvana- In the Buddhist context it refers to the imperturbable stillness of mind after the fires of desire, aversion and delusion have been finally extinguished.

(37)

The Mirrors

Can you just imagine
A world, without mirrors?
The nasty thing
That reminds about
The past and the future
The birth and the corpse.

(38)

Transcendent the Humanity

Transcendent the humanity
Merge with machines, the movie
Of science mythology, pave the
Way to my mind towards the
Creation of a duplicate world
That will not experience natural
Death that we all encounter,

The death is the limitation
For our knowledge and wisdom
The knowledge of exploring the
Falseness of knowledge
Gathered by people that have been
Limited to only one generation
Limited to a single life span
In average of seventy six years,

The wealth can be gathered
Generations from father to child
The knowledge can be written
In books and e-books, and pass
It to the next in future, but the
Wisdom of human brain can not be
Passed it ends in every death,
And it is one of the greatest barriers
For mankind, in the process of

Development in any valued subject
If Aristotle, Da Vinci and Einstein
Can still live and continue their
Creativity, what amazing discoveries
Will there be for generations,

But man has to be decayed and gone
And be packed in heaven in line
Within the stores of mighty Gods' land
Or could come back in another form
Of life in the process of reincarnation
But leaving all the previous knowledge,

But can the wisdom to be continued
Well, if such can to be protected?
There were, are and will be supermen
And women within us, but all
We know is that there is no such
Process of preservation of wisdom
As in the said movie of science,

All theories that have been formed
Available for the man to be misguided
In his journey for winning the universe
Towards a single goal that is to
Exploit the liberal thinking of man.
Inadvertently, unknowingly or unintentionally
Breaking the back bone of man
Doping him for self salvation in another birth.

Transcendence – It is a 2014 science fiction film. The main character Dr. Will Caster is the foremost researcher in the filed of artificial intelligence, working to create a sentient- machine that combines the collective intelligence of everything ever knows with the full range of human emotions.

(39)

The Love

Looking at him I remember the past
The past of a life, a kind of irony of life
The contentment of life is made of
Whatever give and take in these
Events that are periodically occurring,

It is true that history of a man's life
Repeats at every decade or quarter
But one cannot enjoy its fruits
For his body has been decaying
And does not feel the same sweetness
Or bitterness when time passes by
From the day of his formation, and
Commences counting his days of living
Then grows the passiveness of thinking
And finding contentment in life,

At one stage he cries for true love
The other he despises even the source
Of it, in other stages he cries for power
Then he despises its torment for not
Letting him get out,

At one stage he tries to escape
From where he believes he has stagnated
The other day he finds it's all the same
Nothing is immune from final desperation
Of a thinking but not an analytical man,

At one stage he hates fellow humans
The other, he loves them deeply
All mankind in the world, the love
For humanity is the beginning of a new
Era of one's thinking,

Without such love for mankind
Any form of creativeness cannot be
Expected, he can be creative of even in
Killing by inventing different kind of
Killing machines, may be to kill at least
Aliens! or viruses such as HIV, Ebola . . . ,

He can be creative in arts, science, and
Politics, but at all times he has to be
Truly in love with mankind
It is the foundation of the future of our race,

But strongly not the love for a self
Salvation offering at a temple, a church,
A mosque or a *kovil* wherever it sells
If he buys it that invites impliedly him to

Live the rest of his life in a zombie land
A land of living dead, hoping for an
Unknown destination fabricated in a
Sweet fairy tale just like in the tale
of the *Wizard of Oz.*

Wizard of Oz – Savior of the Emarald City, a character in the 1900 novel,
"The wonderful wizard of Oz" by L. Frank Baum.

Kovil – is a Hindu temple in Sri Lanka.

(40)

The Truth

Having removed a cyst in the brain
He lost half of his senses and memory
A part of the *rupakaya* is removed
The relative part of the *arupakaya*
Is also gone,

I compare him to a machine
Oh! but poorly manufactured
Spare parts are hardly available,

Never feel a life as a misery
It's only a battle to be won
Never give up and accept the *status quo*
Never postpone matters until the next birth
There is no time to loose
Since there will be no such second chance,

Brito and *Monika* due to their deep love
So negative to face reality
Fear of barriers in life
Jumped from the world's end
And died clasping their bloody hands
Hoping to get together in the next birth,

Thousands taken away by the sea waves
Why you have not been protected

If you were protected, why this discrimination
From the others who killed in vain,
Probabilities and coincidences are there
Never misinterpret them as
God's power, *karma* or fate,

In youth you must enjoy
While you live with maturity
You must be happy and contented
With what you gained in life
In the end you must go
Just as you came
Until then keep in mind
This machine should run.

Rupakaya and arupakaya – according to Buddhist philosophy the human body consists of two parts, the visible part and the invisible part, the mind. The rupakaya is the visible part and the arupakaya is the invisible part.

Brito and Monika – In early 1970's these two lovers committed suicide together by jumping at World's End, a deep canyon in Sri Lanka.

(41)

Killing of a Self

Poorest soul why did thou kill thyself
I see the faded flower caskets
At the burial lonely facing down
Why tell us all?
The melancholy thee felt
The grief that tortured thy brain cells
What finality and a boldness,
Well! One would say
A mad decision to end thy existence,

Thee has gone leaving already
Available thy quota of oxygen
Well some living being will consume it
Thou hast lost the balance
In the life span of a human
Didn't thou have a blind faith for a God
Or fear for an unforgivable sin
That is to be compensated beyond
At least to survive in this struggle,

End of the day I too would pass
But definitely having consumed
My quota, and with a great
Contentment of winning a battle
Indeed! A fair one.

(42)

The Sinner

Why this untimely invitation!
At one of the most unexpected days
At your wish I was sent and bred
To become a youth and a man
In my harvesting time of life, I have been
Grateful together with a family giving
Us such with utmost respect,
Every day we prayed to you giving
Back our gratitude in return,

Still the kids are to be fed, wife is
Feeble and sick, hence I have to work
Hard as you have cursed to struggle
With the soil and earn my bread to
Feed them and before every meal
We pray with utmost faith and love,

Why you have sent me for by this untimely
Manner, leaving them behind at their
Needy hour, when they are well protected
In my caring, why these venomous cells
Eating my body as well as the soul,

Day by day every limb is filled with filth
Tomorrow I die being ugly and stinking,
In every second death whispers
Your unkind invitation unto my soul
I am in utmost pain for loss of faith,

It was you who has imposed
This duty to breed and feed
Now you are unjustly dismissing
Me from my duties betraying me
At death's hand serving summons
Back to eternity, in your paradise,

Let me finish my unfilled duty towards
My innocent descendants
Do not let them question you
My Lord, you may shut the doors of paradise
Send me any curse or any harsh imprisonment
In your or his hell or wherever you wish
After giving me a full quota of life to be with
My kids and their mother, Well
As I was said your children as well as
My most adorable companions.

(43)

Pray for Thy Betterment

Ye, yonder live with the black dust
Unhealthy and poor, head to foot
Having no roof overhead
Having no cloth around
Having no food to consume
But giving birth to sick
Having them crawling over
Yipping in poisonous mud
Full of all the viruses of the world,

Ye pray for thy betterment
In thy afterlife in heaven
Or in thy re-incarnation
Having encountered with all riches
For a feature like a Goddess
With a king and a kingdom
Having many a children
To be tamed and ruled happily,

Ye have sinned in thy pre-births
And now become poor in order of
karma, and suffer for food and shelter
Thy children suffer for their sins
In the past as well,
They have duly been sent by the utmost
Sophisticated and well updated

Data entry system of thy creators
And protectors of the System,

Ye sleep at the edge of the road
Across the pavement obstructing
The elegant and well mannered
With soft ears for songs of the nightingale
And fresh noses for the fragrance of roses
Ye do behold them with fear and respect
At rich and beautiful who had done only good
Deeds, indeed in their pre-births and
now enjoying the fruits of their endeavour.

(44)

Contentment

Closing the worn out pages
Of my diary, I have sat before
A new page without any
Memories of you,

The tree opposite the window
Is full of tender leaves
Ready to give birth to spring
The breeze touches the skin
Underneath my ears
Giving memories of childhood
The tears have dried
The mind has faded
I am smiling in the present
And inquiring deep within me,

"for how long can I live?"
I already knew the answer
"a very short time indeed"
Then I have muttered to myself
"well then be busy
'tis the happiest
And the most valuable".

(45)

The Quota

The home that does not exist
The village that became a town
The pet cat dead and buried
A long time back, the doll perished
Somewhere in the backyard
The childhood that never comes again
Parents in eternal sleep on their graves . . .
It is true that life is short
The joyous youth is shorter,
I wandered alone the carpeted roads
That lead to so called prosperity
Endless hopes of the urbanized man
Crossed with such annoyance
I felt for eagerness of searching for
My true mates leaving for a while
In this man made crystal world
Amazingly I had no roots of the past
Where should I go, backwards?

I have been looking for a butterfly
At least a charming little one
Oh! I still remember the huge green spider
With his enormous and beautiful web
Where have you gone my friends?
Everything and the being have been decayed
Or gone, reluctantly and silently paving the way

Unto an unknown future generation
Can anybody and anything be eternal?

The lusty green trees, butterflies and the spider
Can anything be non extinct?
If so how the offspring has to grow up and mature
Everything has a quota to live and breed
The tree leaves fluttering with the breeze
Nightingale sings hiding in a beautiful
Moonlit night, and we are all merry dancing,
Singing and drinking, doing nothing worth
But consuming the said quota . . .

The Mind

The mind has no control
Does it require to be packed tightly,
Rigid and solid?
Or to float free like thin air
Everywhere,

It is within your parameters
Of life experience or readings
Or what you heard,
Five senses create
Its movements, it cannot go far,

Mind is a storing component
It stores every stimulation
Of five senses as perceived
The said perception is stored
And creates your attitudes,

The only matter in the human brain is
Too much for him to explore, hence
The best is to give it mysterious
And super form, and make
Nutritious theories on it,

It has gone far in eastern philosophies
It condemns the other body parts
In the biological process of making
Energy, the waste they despise utmost
And treat the human body as full of filth,

This is a machine, it takes fuel
And make energy and waste both
This is a great injustice causing to
Other organs of the body by one
Being ambiguous naming as soul,

Let the mind be mischievous
Its freedom is the righteous,
In this world of three dimensions
Tamed mind is a caged bird
With healthy feathers of no use,

The mind is a water overflowing
In a fountain in a virgin forest
Free to run everywhere, giving
One's life a full quota
Of consummation.

(47)

The Rain, the Same One

The rain, the same one
When deep sleep in my childhood
Embracing the pillow at my side
Covering whole body with a blanket,

The rain, the same one
When I place my child to sleep
At the cot swaying it with
My melodies of love,

The rain, the same one
Feeble I lay, having no hope
In life and counting days
For the departure,

The soft greenery lit in sunlight,
The fluttering of butterflies
With colors of tender spring,
The meekness of a rabbit
And a squirrel who shares the light
Of life in the neighborhood,

Where are the mild soft
Raindrops to whisper
My farewell at my departure
Lounge, offering the final
Contentment of the ultimate
Emancipation of a life.

(48)

Death Wish of a Poet

I was half asleep on the white sand
Of the beach, the whispering breeze
Stroking my neck and ankle
Leaving me submerged in
An eternal poetic fountain
I inquired from the waves
For their wonderful songs
Mixed melodies of life and love,

I gazed at the see waves unstopping
Lives of generations of mankind
Infants to children, teens and men
Dust to dust beneath the damp soil
Covered in a wooden box with gloved hands
For an eternal slumber or for an after life?
Is any interim period in between death
And the customary burial?

Likewise, my poetry though little doomed
Questions the eternal beliefs of mankind
Having no belief or fear in mind
I cried for a break of at least another year
To finish my unwritten book of poetry
The best one of mine to be
Finding the secret door of the paradigm
Wherein we all have been imprisoned,

But I feel approaching black tides
Like demons or automated killing machines
killing and destroying all on the land
Sitting at the very edge embracing
Final soft touches of gentle sea waves
I shout at thee, Oh! Mighty *Uranus*,
The sea God, let me live for another year
For enabling me to write the last book of mine,

All my veins and nerves trembled with
The fear of losing anticipation
Failure in writing my final book
Leaving all bonds aside, choosing this
Uninhabited sea shore to plant my seeds of
Poetry and giving birth to a new philosophy
Of life, as the best for my neighbor and for a
Distant unknown friend in a far away land,

I fear not to die; it is for all the forms
Of life in the earth and beyond
But today in this melancholy second
I demand an extra time to live
In spite of hearing a deadly barking
Of a pack of leaping hyenas
which piercing my soul, taking me
From my beautiful poetic world.

(49)

The Crimson Sky

The days pass by and days to come by
Are the memories and anticipations
The nostalgia of the events in the past
Is the value of life, is the energy of living
Tomorrow is the hope for the better,

The crimson sky paints the contentment
Of the evening, do not fear the falling night
The night invites me to the dreams
Embracing an emancipation of a
Contentment of a well behaved life,

Again same routine of habitual action
Until the day dies at the crimson sky.
The flowers I smell, the taste of the wine,
Even a tear that descending down a cheek
Will be the same tomorrow, the value of life,

In a cold morning with slumbering eyes
I might have encountered in the mirror
a new wrinkle on the face, a grey hair over
My forehead, well I was not dismayed
or fear at aging or departing for ever,

Just look at the trees in the garden
The same are growing, aging and dying.
Just look at the cat and the dog
Equally are growing aging and dying
Paving the way for the next to come by,

When I was in youth or middle age
being bed ridden by a short illness
I had the definite and impatient
Hope to be with the daily routines
Of life, in a more effective manner.

Now at the very end of the journey
This may be my endmost illness
The final bed ridden segment of life
But I am in a bliss of contentment
Anticipating the final gift of nature,

Hence, this may be my last
Crimson sky, I lay feebly like a
Vegetable, I cannot look up,
But I feel the most beautiful sunset,
When at sun set, it paints
The desolate sky with the most
Beautiful crimson color,

Hence, I bow down and bid farewell
Mother Nature with all my gratitude
The Sun, Moon and the Stars, Lake
And the Sea Shore, Green Wilderness
And amazing harmony of lives within it,

Who has blessed me with fresh
air to breathe, purest water to drink
abundance of fruit and food,
amazing me with the harmony of
lives of all living beings,

All beings who have simultaneously
Consumed their quota of life, along with
My own limited time segment and I say
Farewell to all my sharers who have
Offered me the contentment of life.

Palitha Ranatunge

Printed in the United States
By the Printers

Printed in the United States
By Bookmasters